Unschooling
Rules

Unschooling Rules

55 Ways to Unlearn What
We Know About Schools
and Rediscover Education

Clark Aldrich

GREENLEAF
BOOK GROUP PRESS

Published by Greenleaf Book Group Press
Austin, Texas
www.gbgpress.com

Distributed by Greenleaf Book Group LLC

For ordering information or special discounts for bulk purchases, please
contact Greenleaf Book Group LLC at PO Box 91869, Austin, TX 78709,
512.891.6100.

Design and composition by Greenleaf Book Group LLC and Alex Head
Cover design by Greenleaf Book Group LLC

Publisher's Cataloging-In-Publication Data

(Prepared by The Donohue Group, Inc.)

Aldrich, Clark, 1967-   Unschooling rules : 55 ways to unlearn what we know
about schools and rediscover education / Clark Aldrich.—2nd ed.   p. ; cm.

   First ed. published as : Unschooling rules : 50 perspectives and insights from
observing homeschoolers and unschoolers on deconstructing schools and
reconstructing education, c2010.

   Includes index.

   ISBN: 978-1-60832-116-2

   1. Education—United States. 2. Schools—United States. 3. Education—Aims
and objectives—United States. 4. Educational change—United States. I. Title.

LB885.A43 U57 2011

371/.00973   2010941059

Part of the Tree Neutral® program, which offsets the number of
trees consumed in the production and printing of this book by
taking proactive steps, such as planting trees in direct proportion
to the number of trees used: www.treeneutral.com

Printed in the United States of America on acid-free paper

11 12 13 14   15 16   10 9 8 7 6 5 4 3 2   Tree Neutral®

Second Edition

Contents

Foreword

If somewhere deep inside you, you suspect there's something wrong with America's educational system, we have something in common.

As a successful entrepreneur and a Socratic teacher for the last twenty years, I've spent a lot of time working in and studying our educational systems. From the halls of Harvard Business School and inside my own classroom, to serving on blue-ribbon educational commissions for the Governor of Texas and working on educational reforms with scores of CEOs, I've worked inside the belly of the beast of education, where most of us aren't allowed to go. It's not a pretty sight.

For years I accepted the paradigm put forward by "Educrats" and worshipped by well-meaning political and business leaders: our K-16 educational system should be organized like a factory, where teachers and administrators busily pour knowledge into the heads of students in order to produce more productive citizens.

Then one day I had a wake-up call. Surprisingly, it didn't come while working on an educational simulation with Clark or meeting with a reform-minded CEO or the Dean of the Harvard Business School, but with an elementary school teacher. And it all revolved around our own children.

My wife and I suspected it might be time to move our six- and seven-year-old boys from a Montessori preschool to a more traditional educational environment. So I asked for a meeting with one of the best teachers at one of the best private elementary schools in Austin, Texas, and asked: "When should we transition our sons to a more traditional system?"

"As soon as possible," he replied. Somewhat taken aback, I asked why.

"Because the longer they are in a nontraditional school, the harder it will be for them to sit still and be lectured to all day."

I pictured our two curious, lively, happy boys chained to a desk for hours on end, and before I could stop myself said, "I don't blame them."

The teacher looked at the floor for the longest time. So long that I thought something was wrong. Then he looked up, with tears in his eyes, and softly said, "I don't either."

That moment, that day, I knew our family was finished with traditional education, destined to join Clark's army of unschoolers. In that instant I saw why the K-16 factory analogy was so flawed, not just conceptually, but morally, too. Because our two beautiful sons aren't widgets. And neither are your children.

Each child has a spark of genius waiting to be discovered, ignited, and fed. And the goal of schools shouldn't be to manufacture "productive citizens" to fill some corporate cubicle; it should be to inspire each child to find a "calling" that will change the world. The jobs for the future are no longer Manager, Director, or Analyst, but Entrepreneur, Creator, and even Revolutionary.

Since my epiphany, I've done a lot of reading and research. I've come to respect how the one-room schoolhouses and apprenticeship programs delivered the basic skills and shaped the characters of leaders like Franklin, Washington, Jefferson, and Lincoln.

I've learned that most of America's inventions and advances haven't come from studying traditional academic theory but from the curiosity and tinkering of mavericks—Galileo, Newton, Einstein, Curie, Edison, and thousands of others.

Perhaps most importantly for my own journey, my wife and I started Acton Academy, a new type of elementary school based on the old one-room schoolhouse but supplemented by the latest in game-based software for delivering basic skills like reading and writing. We heard Clark's call that children should "learn to do" and "learn to be" through exposure to real-world projects, and that this growth would inspire them to "learn to know" even more.

As a result, we've watched perfectly normal students advance 2.5 grade levels in just a ten-month period, and have seen many who didn't want to leave school for our six-week summer break.

So, as you read through this engaging—and even addictive—set of Clark's observations, I ask you to set aside your preconceived notions of school and take in a strong dose of common sense. Open your mind to the idea that the educational "un-system" that made America the greatest country on Earth still has many more lessons to teach.

Let this book serve as your wake-up call, whether you are a parent, a teacher, an administrator, an educational-reformer politician, or a business leader. And when you finish it, I encourage you to read some of the books or to visit some of the websites, programs, and schools I've listed in the afterword. Actually, I hope you will do a lot more. Maybe you'll even decide to join this purposely disorganized, rich, colorful, noisy band of unschoolers yourself.

Because education—real education—matters a lot.

Jeff Sandefer
Winter 2010

Introduction

To many, learning in a classroom is like eating food from the frozen section of a supermarket. What initially appears to be sustaining, convenient, and diverse is really overprocessed, expensive, and homogeneous.

It's not surprising why. Schools today are stuck in a rut.

In many schools across the world, children *en masse* get dropped off and enter buildings where they become the recipient of linear "teaching" and tests. They go home, do homework, and start over again the next day—all for the goal of preparing them for the next level of school and meeting broad and dubiously constructed standards.

The consequences of this single approach are huge. It is reasonable to assume that for 95 percent of all students, their experience in K-12 schools will not significantly change in the next 30 years.

Few even question this pattern anymore, but the education landscape is nevertheless finally getting some diversity. Just as followers of Michael Pollan are no longer relying on the industrial food complex to provide them their sustenance, so too are a growing number of homeschoolers and unschoolers questioning the assumptions of today's industrial education system.

These homeschoolers and unschoolers are families that have decided not to partake in today's K-12 school system because they, using a variety of calculations, believe the costs outweigh the benefits. They are striving to evolve new approaches, not from the once-removed vantage of politicians or board members or even smart individuals grinding through the Sisyphean task of trying to get a few policies changed, but by abandoning the model and starting over. Almost exclusively, they currently represent education's real research and development.

Perhaps the hardest part of this revolution for parents to overcome, however, is realizing just how ingrained the traditional school habits of teaching children truly are. Homeschoolers and unschoolers have to adopt the genuine best practices of schools while leaving behind ineffective legacy processes and industrial conceits, in place of which they must fill in the gaps.

This book, whose name is both an oxymoron and a double entendre, is the result of my research to identify and frame the guidelines that these home- and unschoolers are uncovering in childhood education. To best present them, *Unschooling Rules* is organized according to what I call the Seven Cs of Education:

- *Curricula*: The selection
- *Content*: The pieces
- *Coaching*: The adult
- *Customization*: The flexibility
- *Community*: The peers
- *Credit*: The documentation
- *[Day] Care*: The place

It is time to consider new approaches to education through a lens outside the ones of the education-industrial complex. The landscape is finally changing. And not a moment too soon.

Author's promise: This book does not contain slews of inspirational quotes about the importance of education and change, nor ones about the problems of the current system. If these types of quotes worked, (a) schools would already have changed, and (b) schools wouldn't have to change.

Part One: Curricula

1

·····································

Learn to be; learn to do; learn to know.

There are three different types of learning: *learning to be*, *learning to do*, and *learning to know*.

Learning to be focuses on helping someone understand who they are and who they want to be. This type of learning answers such questions as: "What do I love doing?" "What is my dream?" "What gives me energy?" "What are my unique strengths?" and even "What is my role in a group?" Reflection is necessary. Online social networking (such as Facebook) has exploded in part because it partially meets this need. Learning to be is the most individualistic of the three different types of learning.

Learning to do, in contrast, focuses on developing skills that can be applied, such as in the productive world. Learning to do almost always involves significant *practice*. Learning to do topics include such abstract skills as leadership, innovation, stewardship, and project management on one end, and more literal skills, such as how to build, grow, use, or fix things, on the other.

Learning to know focuses on knowledge that can be captured in books and lectures. This includes timelines and dates, definitions and facts. Google and Wikipedia are the ultimate learning to know tools. Most schools are very busy at developing this type of learning.

Any curriculum that focuses solely on one of these types of learning is missing most of the opportunities for complete learning. Further, there is a logical order to presenting the three different types. Traditional schools' forte, *learning to know*, can come only after *learning to be* and *learning to do* have successfully begun.

It is the role of childhood to build these three types of learning into every individual. Society pays a steep price when people are not developed in all areas.

But let's start somewhere comfortable . . .

2

....

Focus on reading, writing, and arithmetic.

Our grandparents got it right. The core curriculum for academic-style content is simply *reading, writing,* and *arithmetic.*

Which leads to the next rule . . .

3

....

Learn something because you need it or because you love it.

There are two reasons to learn something: either because you need it or because you love it. Nevertheless, needed content must be approached differently from loved content.

The content one *needs to know* is fairly focused. From the traditional curricula, one needs to know reading, writing, and arithmetic. What one needs to know should also include areas such as stewardship, project management, innovation, and security. This content is relatively consistent across populations.

And then there are the things that one loves. Here, learning is automatic.

What one loves is highly individualistic. For some, this may include music. For others, it may be truck engines. Or clothes. Or movies. Or growing food. Or advanced robotics. Or classics of literature. Or astronomy charts. Or dinosaurs.

In this age of the Internet, the rigorous pursuit of our passions (sometimes lifelong, sometimes extinguished even before the conclusion of the first YouTube video we watch) is now infinitely possible.

The bloating of most curricula comes from a simple flaw. Each generation believes that what they *love* the next generation *needs*.

Meanwhile, there still are . . .

4

....

Twenty-five critical skills are seldom taught, tested, or graded in high school.

So many important *learning to do* skills simply fall through the cracks of traditional schools. Here are some skills, both simple and complex, that should be essential for any accredited high school curricula:

- Adapting
- Analyzing and Managing Risks
- Applying Economic, Value, and Governing Models
- Behaving Ethically
- Being a Leader
- Building and Nurturing Relationships
- Communicating

- Creating or Process Reengineering New Actions, Processes, and Tools
- Developing Security
- Efficiently Meeting Complex Needs
- Gathering Evidence
- Identifying and Using Boards of Mentors and Advisers
- Maintaining and Practicing Stewardship of Important Systems and Capabilities
- Making Prudent Decisions
- Managing Conflict
- Managing Projects
- Negotiating
- Planning Long Term
- Prioritizing Tasks and Goals
- Probing
- Procurement
- Scheduling
- Solving Problems Innovatively
- Sourcing/Buying Goods and Services
- Using Containment Strategies

These we should strive to teach our children and young adults. In contrast . . .

5

....

Don't worry about preparing students for jobs from an Agatha Christie novel.

Schools seem disproportionately intent on enabling children to uncover their potential in professions that are staggeringly unlikely, low paying, and about a hundred years past their peak. For example, educators place great attention and ethical value on the jobs of:

- The novelist—thus everyone studies techniques used to create great literature.
- The musician—thus everyone is made to play an instrument.
- The professional mathematician—thus everyone is pushed into a calculus track (even if they never reach it).

Of course, diverse exposure is part of a rich life. If

children love any of these, let them embrace them. If a student loves and embraces playing an instrument, that is great during "class time."

But in terms of pushing archaic areas of study to prepare them for life as though they were in a Jane Austin or Agatha Christie novel, forget about it.

And while we are on this topic . . .

6

....

Avoid the academic false dichotomy of "The Cultural Literacy Track" or "The Vocational Track."

Many school programs seem to offer either The Cultural Literacy Track or The Vocational Track.

- The Cultural Literacy programs are designed for the "smart kids" who are going to go on to ever-higher levels of both education and financial success. This track, with no pretense of being real world, includes classes on classics, foreign languages, and math theory (such as calculus). It is a curriculum based on "teach what has been taught."

- The Vocational programs are for the "remedial kids" who are going to have only blue-collar futures if they are in high school (taking classes such as wood working) or inflexible paraprofessional paths if they are in college (such as degrees in physical therapy).

This two-tier approach is an immoral sorting system with crippling consequences. Maybe worse, it also presents a false dichotomy. Instead, true wisdom comes from a synthesis of those two perspectives and more.

The best example of bringing together the application of real skills and big ideas comes at the graduate level, such as with law, medicine, business, and engineering. Which is great—but why pay for 15 years of hobbling schooling before an individual gets there?

Part Two: Content

7

....

Throughout life, everyone unschools most of the time.

When a doctor finds a rarely seen condition in a patient, she does not sign up for a class that covers the material, but will run for 6 weeks and start the following semester.

When faced with evidence of a toxic sedimentation crisis, the politician does not apply to a prestigious university's environmental policy master's degree program.

When the director of a nonprofit organization sees an opportunity to expand into a foreign country, his first instinct is not to review old MBA course notes.

All people unschool to learn most of their knowledge during most of their lives. The only variables are how well do they do it, and when do they start.

Meanwhile . . .

8

················

What a person learns in a classroom is how to be a person in a classroom.

The teacher might be talking about history or math, but what the students in a traditional classroom are learning is how to be students in a classroom.

And they are learning it very well.

They are learning how to take notes. They are learning how to surreptitiously communicate with peers. They are learning how to ask questions to endear themselves to authority figures.

It is impressive, on one level, that we spend billions of dollars and innumerable hours creating this perfect, practice-based environment in which children's abilities to sit still in classrooms are honed. Furthermore, we have built a reward structure to praise those students who can sit in classrooms better than anyone else. We let them run our planet.

However, given that this model is economically running economies into the ground and obesity is a global epidemic, it may be time to collectively build and reward different skills. Learning is a full contact sport. To learn something new, a student has to *do* something new and often *be* somewhere new.

Rather than viewing and treating students who want to *do* something new as troublemakers who need to be fixed, we should recognize that they will be the engines of improvements in our standard of living. Point of fact, they always have been.

To make things worse . . .

9

Sitting through a classroom lecture is not just unnatural for most people, it is painful.

Sitting through a classroom lecture is painful for most people most of the time. We all know this, yet so many deny it or view it as a personal failing.

When human beings are required to sit and listen, we squirm. We watch the clock tick slowly. Minutes can seem like hours.

We escape into our own head. We invent activities to either occupy or numb ourselves. The most talented classroom sitters create micro-tasks to busy their hands and the other 80 percent of their minds.

The pain is cumulative. The first hour of lecture in a day is bearable. The second is hard. The third is white-hot excruciating. The highly engaging presenter who periodically arises in the classroom does little to soften the physiological impact of the subsequent dull one.

This reality goes beyond a *power* thing, or even an *interest* thing, or a *quality of the teacher* thing. Even when corporate leaders and heads of state attend highly relevant daylong events at which they listen to the highest-tier speakers, they are suppressing their own body ticks 90 minutes into the lecture. The lunch break becomes an oasis.

Students are psychologically ravished daily by this onslaught. And it is costly on all involved—teachers, administrators, parents, siblings.

Although this recommendation subverts most industrial business and logistics models, 2 non-adjacent hours of lecture a day should be the greatest number for any institution or program. And the most successful will have even less than that.

This requires an alternative approach. Start by embracing the idea that . . .

10

....

Animals are better than books about animals.

Children should have as much exposure as possible to animals. In all animals, including domestic, farm, and wild, are entire curricula. There are biology, sociology, genetics, economics, history, cultures, communication, language, hierarchies, governance, relationships sweeping story arcs, morality, even nutrition, just to name a few. Animals are the perfect microcosms. They are life.

But it doesn't count if the animals are just images or characters in a book. A poster of a kitten clinging to a branch with the words "Hang in there!" doesn't count either. There is no greater example of the "flattening of content" that classes achieve than a "unit study" that examines, even purports to love, animals but does not actually engage any on a regular basis.

Worse still, the more removed a culture is from animals, the more stylized and inaccurately the animals are inevitably represented. Tribes in Africa portray hippos as the deadly, fierce creatures they are. By the time most schoolchildren see them in the United States, they have morphed into "Mr. Hippo gets in his car to drive to work," complete with his bright pink skin and marshmallow-shaped teeth.

Dogs and cats, chickens and cows, songbirds and frogs are all there, waiting to be engaged. They have so much to teach us that any attempt to segregate environments of learning from them should never be accepted.

In fact . . .

11

....

Use microcosms as much as possible in learning programs.

Microcosms are self-contained models of larger and more complex systems. Lessons learned, including what are good things to do and good results to get, can be transferred to the bigger productive world.

Examples of microcosms that can be used in education include, among others:

- Fish tanks
- Lemonade stands and bake sales
- Gardens
- One-person businesses
- Team sports

Emerging technology has also put more power at the fingertips of everyone. A 12-year-old can now:

- Do blog reporting on local news

- Plan a trip to any location, down to budgets, flight times, and hotels

Microcosms should be used as often as possible. Why? Because, among the many other advantages, the projects require stewardship; cramming is not possible; and the results are authentic and self-evident.

Going one step further . . .

12

Internships, apprenticeships, and interesting jobs beat term papers, textbooks, and tests.

The educational needs of older children are better met by time spent on internships, in apprenticeships, or at interesting jobs rather than writing ever longer reports, memorizing more passages from textbooks, completing longer math proofs, or taking ever more complex tests. Some of the best places where students could look to work and learn are:

- On a local political campaign
- On a farm
- At a museum
- For a radio or television news station
- At a newspaper
- In a bakery

- In a hospital
- In park or trail maintenance
- At an environmental foundation
- With a police or fire department

Many jobs can be appropriate for short-term (1- to 3-month) projects. Just look for places where people really care about the finished job.

This leads to the ability and passion to . . .

13

....

Include meaningful work.

Everyone needs to do meaningful work. That is a *sine que non* of life.

Meaningful work is objectively valued by others. It is more of the "Thank you for shoveling my walk" variety than the "Hey, what a pretty picture of a butterfly you finger-painted" or even "Great job scoring that winning point" kind of way.

The challenge is finding the appropriate tasks calibrated to the individual's skill level. Recycling, cleaning out stalls, cooking food for others, taking care of neighbors' pets, setting up a friend's computer network, and creating a homepage are all possibilities.

This meaningful work is the best of way of learning. In fact, long-term learning may be impossible to achieve in any other type of environment.

But don't forget . . .

14

....

Create and use periods of reflection.

A critical part of the learning process is time for quiet reflection about activities—both before and after they are undertaken. So the busier children are the less they may actually be learning.

The amount of time required to process thoughts, as well as the perceived "rawness" of the experience, varies considerably from person to person. It could be that for 1 "average" hour of stimulation, people need an hour of reflection to create useful memories. On occasion, it might be much more than that; for example, it could easily require 10 or 15 hours or more to process 1 intense hour of unfamiliar activity, especially one that's well outside of one's comfort zone.

One example here is a vacation tour. We spend a frantic week in a foreign city, packing in as much as possible, seeing new monuments and trying new foods.

But it is only over subsequent weeks, months, even years that, often through looking at photographs of the sights and talking to people who accompanied us on the trip, we "unpack" the experience and sort it out. The lessons learned come much later. (Although prework here, such as reading travel guides or viewing travelogues, as with other examples, can sometimes lessen the need for post-trip processing.)

A more neurological example is rapid eye movement (REM) sleep. During this deep phase of the sleeping process, people sort out the memories of the day. When people are deprived of REM sleep, they don't process experiences correctly into memory. They often become irritable and easily confused as a result.

"School days" should have extensive downtimes—that is, stretches without scheduled activities and even without the context of impending homework. Admittedly, one of the scariest things for all of us is to be alone with our thoughts. But it is ultimately scarier not to be.

Meanwhile . . .

15

....

If you care about learning, start with food.

How a school (or any other place of learning) views food sheds a lot of light on how it views education.

Though predictable and cost-effective in the short run, mass-produced, highly processed, standardized, low-cost, and packaged products that are engineered and marketed centrally and shipped out to be reconstituted at their point of use do not work. This is as true with food (such as frozen hamburgers prepared by cafeteria workers) as educational experiences (such as textbooks and curricula presented by teachers).

This comparison is much more than just a semantic flourish. Consider that:

- Food is a perfect microcosm of learning. Anyone who does not eat well has failed in his or her own ability to systematically learn.

- Learning is impossible without being fed. The act of growing according to one's genetic blueprint supersedes the act of learning. Students who are adding inches to their height are biologically different from people who are not, and the same eating schedule will not accommodate both.

- Every stated goal of an educational institution (or real goal of a parent) is predicated on a student's lifelong health, which requires good food as a foundation.

Given this, almost any school can be evaluated by the simple act of observing lunchtime. So learning environments—accreditation bodies take note—be they public, private, or home, must include the highest-quality food in order to be credible.

And at the other end of the spectrum . . .

16

Embrace all technologies.

Educators should completely embrace technology. Smartphones, Twitter, blogs, Skype, and Facebook (plus dozens more to come) are the context of learning and being productive for decades to come. A spell-checker frees us up from memorization and, thus, spelling tests.

If a traditional school situation is disrupted by new technology, nine times out of ten it is the school situation that needs to be changed, not the access to technology. Schools hate the fluidity of technology. But students love it, need it, and will find a way to use it.

For example . . .

17

·······································

Listen while doing.

Where appropriate and available, consider introducing podcasts and unabridged recordings of books as healthier alternatives to using the same old classroom lectures and printed media. Any part of a classroom activity that can be replaced by a recording should be. Where instructors are involved, they should be coaching, not presenting.

The corollary is also true. These recordings can be engaged while a person is driving, working out, even doing chores or other jobs that don't require extreme concentration.

And a different technology enables . . .

18

One computer + one spreadsheet software program = math curricula.

Math must be part of a critical core curriculum. It is one of the few subjects, along with reading and writing, worth making mandatory. No one should enter the productive world, nor can they make good life decisions, without a deep and comfortable experience with math.

Given that, what math should be taught? Most math curricula have been hopelessly tangled up in a quagmire of precedent, prestige, and capriciousness. Consequently, areas like long division, geometry, and calculus are overemphasized. And areas like discrete math, logic, programming, permutations, probabilities, and combinatorics are deemphasized.

(For most students, calculus should be covered in history classes, if at all. It is a towering invention in the same vein as the potter's wheel or the loom.)

Obviously there are people who are passionate about math, and some of them go on to be pure or applied math or engineering majors. For them, calculus is required.

However, there remains a perfect tool and context for math for the many people who do not share that passion. And that is a good spreadsheet, which can be created with Microsoft Excel, which many people have on their computers.

- The built-in math functions of a spreadsheet have accurately captured a range of abilities necessary for planners, decision makers, and scientists to use.

- Further, the program still requires rigorous high-level planning and programming. A spreadsheet does a lot of the rote work, but it is still simply developing the rock solid conceptualization and understanding of the material on the part of the user.

- Students can solve the same problem in different ways, which is a plus for reactance-inflicted teenagers (although bad for traditional teachers).

- Finally, spreadsheets allow for accessing information visually through symbols as well as graphs. Will Wright, the brilliant creator of *SimCity* and *The Sims*, mused in a conversation we had if it wouldn't be better initially for a person to teach math without showing any numbers at all!

Using a spreadsheet well, and being able to use as many of the built-in equations as possible in the appropriate situation and to the right end, is a better framework than the textbooks and worksheets and obscure topics of yesteryear.

Audiobooks and spreadsheets are just some of the materials at hand if you . . .

19

....

Have a well-stocked library.

Places that encourage formal learning should have a well-stocked library. Few moments are more satisfying than having a child walk up to a shelf and pull out something perfect.

But in this day and age, it should not just be references and the classics that adorn the shelves.

Libraries should also include other media:

- DVDs/Blu-rays of great movies, documentaries, and television series

- Picture books of geographical locations and art

- Computer games such as those produced by the *SimCity* and *Civilization* franchises

- Maps, which should also be on each library's own walls

- Organized personal photographs, home movies, and scrapbooks

Of course, the Internet is the ultimate repository. But the tangibility and portability of local copies of great or otherwise relevant works might make them the most enticing and see to it that they are utterly consumed.

When assembling a library, don't forget that students should . . .

20

Read what normal people read.

Reading is a core skill. Everyone needs to know how to do it pretty well.

But the good news is that words are everywhere. The Internet has a lot of them. So do books, magazines, newspapers, stores, even on-screen computer game instructions. It is not hard to find words that are relevant, helpful, even powerful.

So, with all of the words around, why does the education-industrial complex exaggerate the use of specialized, standardized schoolbooks? Consider these two categories alone:

- *Textbooks*, which are the content equivalent of frozen TV dinners—highly processed and "complete."

- *Classics* such as *Wuthering Heights*, which are not only taught year after year but also often enough by teachers who enhance the

lessons by sharing experiences from their
own high school classes decades earlier

This standardization, of course, enables tests that
can be used across broad populations and, over the
years, to measure how much the students remembered.

Which means that these processes make sense if
you look at schools as factories (with an expected 30-
year lifespan of the equipment) but not if you think of
students as individuals. Using materials that are more
relevant, more diverse, more self-selected, more helpful, and more current make for better reading.

And speaking of reading . . .

21

Is it better to be "A Great Reader" than "Addicted to Computer Games"?

As a whole, most people are pretty comfortable assigning moral virtue to lots of reading and moral turpitude to playing lots of computer games. In truth, the two activities are about equal. From a cultural and "useful in development" perspective, the best of each medium are of comparable worth to a student today. Likewise, each has its terrible examples.

Books offer the following advantages:

- Developing empathy more effectively through presentations of inner monologues
- Presenting facts
- Having a lengthy body of analysis around

them, which makes teaching them pretty
easy

- Relying far less on violence
- Exposing people to brilliant writing styles
- Representing the oldest accessible art form
  of our culture

Computer games, in contrast, have the advantage
of being active content. Computer games develop skills
and new awareness, requiring the resolution of frustra-
tion. In addition, they often are group activities. They
provide an overall better microcosm of learning.

Any computer game is also a medium of its time, at-
tracting the current generation of great artists. Modern-
day Shakespeares or Miltons will be game designers.

Having said that, however, both computer games
and books are still self-referential. This is a problematic
quality if either format is consumed beyond modera-
tion. Accessing art should never be framed as an inher-
ently worthwhile activity. It is only morally good if it
leads to morally good actions.

The right computer games and other technology
make it easier to . . .

22

....

Formally learn only what is reinforced during the next 14 days (you will forget everything else anyway).

This rule is very simple. Formally learn only what is reinforced in the productive world in the next 14 days. There are two reasons for this.

First, it keeps a formal curriculum from spiraling out of control into the highly theoretical, legacy, or adult pet projects.

Second, knowledge (and especially *learning to know*) decays quickly. So even if you do learn something theoretically interesting, unless it is reinforced, you will forget most of it anyway.

Teachers often say, "It is frustrating when students come back from vacation, because they have forgotten everything." What they intend as a shared complaint is a sweeping and devastating critique of the entire school system.

Now, a great result of the philosophy to teach only what will be used immediately in the real world is that it should not simply impact what is formally learned, it should also encourage more activities, be they *meaningful work* or *microcosms*. For example, math that is taught should be subsequently applied to managing a budget for a project and writing techniques that are demonstrated in class are employed in blogging news articles.

One way to summarize is . . .

23

....

Build more, consume less.

Those leading the education-industrial system have two incompatible goals:

On the one hand, they are ever more following the dated and disproved top-down "management" theories of metrics, standardization, and short-term accountability.

On the other hand, those at the national level who track skills, because they are terrified at the drop in mathematics and science competencies in today's students, are trying to change schools to better develop our nation's capabilities in these disciplines.

The truth here is that for schools, getting out of the way may be the best thing they can do. Students, left alone, will build things. They will create unique, surprising ways to meet specific needs that often only they understand (even if the need is to enable an elaborate prank).

Building can be done with computer code or lumber or ingredients or fabric. And building is the opposite of consuming, which is done with movies, textbooks, restaurant meals, most video games, or lectures.

The next generation of engineers and scientists are not going to be the ones who are the best "students" who memorize a given week's lists of tables and equations before heading off to history class where they do the same with historical figures and dates. In fact, it will be a failing graduate school that draws from this lot. The next generation of engineers and scientists will be the ones who are skipping the class but painfully and meticulously gathering the building blocks in their secret workshop and putting together something unprecedented.

Part Three: Coaching

24

Teaching is leadership.
Most teaching is bad leadership.

The process of educating entails leadership. The word "education" is from the Latin word for "to lead forth," just as the word "pedagogy" is from the Greek word "to lead."

The specific *type* of leadership style an educator uses, however, results in predictable, different, but not always considered implications.

When a coercive technique is used (a "directive" leadership style), such as lecturing to students, mandating that pupils follow a specific process, or making young learners prepare for and take a traditional test, short-term target behavior only will be exhibited.

You get a positive blip in test scores, but *without any long-term impact*. In fact, ordering people to do something often results in the *opposite long-term behavior or belief system*.

When students are given freedom (a "participative"

or "collaborative" leadership style) in responsive environments, a better effect occurs. When they are allowed to create their own theories or even entire curricula, students' long-term behaviors are aligned with what they discover and refine.

One way to lead well is to . . .

25

....

Expose more, teach less.

Children should be exposed to as much richness as possible. This includes different philosophies, different cultures, different art forms, different careers, and different forms of meaningful work.

Here are some guidelines to ensure successful exposure to rich variety.

Do:

- Travel. While this can seem to imply a big trip, it shouldn't. It is amazing how much is available within a 1-hour car-drive radius of almost everyone's community.

- Talk intimately to authentic experts. Find the people who care more and know more and do more (people who have studied more don't count). Engage them one-on-one if possible.

- Observe experts in their environment, doing what they do best.

- Be flexible according to a child's interest. Require that the child remain a few minutes, but then be equally prepared to leave quickly or stay all day.

Don't:

- Use a standardized checklist. There should never be an "approved" list of subjects for early-life stimulation (although many have pushed for foreign languages and high culture such as art, history, or music). The reasons for this are many, including that there are just too many potential areas, and one has to be flexible when the right opportunities arise.

- Subvert the experience with directive-style teaching techniques. There should never be a test or paper required after an exposure event, for example. These extrinsic motivation techniques overshadow any nascent and emerging interest.

Meanwhile, beware that the use of media or highly staged events is a double-edged sword. Where tickets are involved, exposure-based interests are *seldom* born. Movies, museums, Broadway performances, air shows, fairs, and sporting events can be used as a last resort and solely where they do not break the guidelines outlined in this rule.

From a productivity and management perspective, exposure is wasteful in the short run; it is essential, however, in the very long run.

For example, exposing a child to a great scientist has a low probability of predictably pushing him or her down a science path. But over the years, any child leading a life of rich exposure will predictably find what they love and where they can uniquely contribute.

This is part of a greater framework because . . .

26

....

Biologically, the necessary order of learning is: explore, then play, then add rigor.

Look at the process by which children learn to swim.

First, children are introduced to the body of water, be it an ocean, a lake, or a swimming pool. New young swimmers initially (and accurately) perceive the water as a scary, foreign environment. The "educational" challenge at this stage is simply to get them to enter and move around in this strange world. The children may dip their toes in while watching other people, or they may just jump straight in. A parent or teacher may have to coax them in.

Once children get comfortable in the water itself, they naturally start to play. They see how long they can hold their breath; they do flips in the water or scour the bottom. They invent small games or imaginary worlds, or their swim teachers give them broad rules for light games, such as tag. These games start off very casually and tend to become more structured and more complex. Here children get comfortable with the affordances of the world and their role in it.

Finally, the children begin to test themselves through increasingly rigorous rules and specific challenges. They go into deeper water. They learn and practice new and often specific strokes. They try to swim measured lengths underwater. They go from open-ended tag to racing each other. These exercises force them to hone skills they can transfer to other bodies of water.

Children move effortlessly from exploration and free roam to structured but simple games to taking on rigorous challenges. This reality prompts three thoughts.

First, imagine how stunted and crippled and punitive the learning process would be without the exploration and play phases.

Second, imagine how the first two phases would be implemented in a traditional state-run industrial school—with tests and metrics and "teacher and student accountability."

Third, and most importantly, for all ages, be the subject math or biology or business or engineering the greatest challenge for all instructors and coaches is to create situations and learning environments that allow for not one or two but for all three phases to happen.

This and other coaching approaches require some changes. For example . . .

27

The ideal class size isn't thirty, or even fifteen, but more like five.

What is the ideal class size? When listening to popular rhetoric, we are told that twenty-five to thirty-five is really, really bad, and fifteen is really, really good.

While fifteen is better, that's kind of like saying driving 95 mph is better than 125. Anyone who has tried to interact with fifteen children knows the activity is still that of shepherding, and projecting content.

Now ask yourself, if you weren't constrained by budget or logistics or even common sense, what would the ideal class size be?

Really, class size should be about five. This allows common presentations, peer-to-peer conversations, and one-on-one coach-to-student interactions.

Note, incidentally, that with this ideal class size comes a redefinition of class, from "entire community all day" to "time of focused learning."

From the point of view of the education industry, fifteen is a calculated target—a stretch goal for more funding without actually meeting the needs of the students. Once you get past their framing, the ideal number is much different.

In addition, because of this industrial mind-set . . .

28

One traditional school day includes less than 3 hours of formal instruction and practice, which you can cover in 2.

If you look at class schedules and other school propaganda, you might think that (a) the students' entire day is filled with hour after hour of rigorous work, and (b) even more hours are needed. But if you were to follow one student as an anthropologist might, actually keeping track of the time spent under instruction and in practice assignments, the real number is a little less than 3 hours.

For most students, 3 hours of formal work is the most they can absorb anyway. This is an upper limit.

Why, then, are there discussions about having longer school days? Frankly, because lack of time is a universal excuse for bad performance in schools, and it allows for ducking the harder work of examining teaching techniques or curricula. Schools, as any industrial complex, would rather ask for more resources and sell more stuff (in this case, school hours) than change anything. For this reason and others, schools are spectacularly unmotivated to reduce the length of the school day. Given that any work project expands to fill the resources allocated to it, this is a problem.

Thankfully, when working with between one and five students, formal instruction and practice can be much richer, as well as more targeted. Thus 2 structured hours of instruction and practice can cover more content than a full industrial school day.

And if you want students to remember and learn much more than a typical school student, you may decide on even less formal time.

This illuminates why . . .

29

Homework helps school systems, not students.

The education-industrial system is addicted to homework. From a "business" perspective, it meets the needs of a K-12 school perfectly:

- It reduces the responsibility and accountability of the existing teachers and school processes.

- It makes parents accountable to the school, instead of the other way around.

- It keeps the student feeling guilty and unempowered.

- It maintains the illusion that there is so much to teach and the school mission is so important that they are worth consuming all aspects of a child's life.

But the cost is extraordinarily high on the students' education.

Homework:

- Robs children and their families of meaningful time together.

- Robs children of self-paced experiment and reflection time where so much *learning to be*, *learning to do*, and yes, *learning to know* actually occurs. This is where boys and girls, on their own, can learn what they love.

- Covers up bad processes and bloated curricula.

Self-paced projects, especially those involving teams, are powerful and meaningful. But if something cannot be conveyed or scheduled during the school day, it is the people who are in charge that must adapt and reengineer, not the students and their families.

However, to make this effective, we have to realize the truth that . . .

30

....

Every day, adults are role models of learning (whether or not they want to be).

Whatever learning activities adults want children to perform, they have to model themselves. If they want children to read novels, they have to read novels. If they want children to do science experiments, they have to do science experiments. If they want children to write blogs, they have to write blogs.

Being a role model has two values, not necessarily in this order. First, children learn by watching adults. Second, adults will be a lot more thoughtful in what they assign children to do if they actually have to do it themselves.

If you do this you will . . .

31

Avoid the Stockholm syndrome.

The premise of the future of education has to be that parents and students will be able to choose from a variety of models. Ironically, today's lack of choice makes some parents of children in school systems both more supportive of a single school approach and less convincing to others. A single school approach is one where parents have no real choice (or believe they have no real choice) when it comes to school options for their children. Parents in this mind-set can (and do) adamantly argue how great their one option is, but in a way this falls flat.

This is due in part to a situation reminiscent of the *Stockholm syndrome.* The Stockholm syndrome occurs when victims, who are under the total control of a few all-powerful people, develop sympathy toward their captors. This phenomenon has been identified from studying hostage situations.

Similarly (but obviously less extreme), some students and parents form an emotional bond with the teachers and institutions that have enormous control over their lives and futures. This goes beyond mere rationalizing or buying in.

The less choice some parents and students (believe that they) have, the more they praise these institutions. And yet, these same parents and students cry with joy and relief at graduation ceremonies and have nightmares about schools the rest of their lives.

Thankfully, as an appreciation for the varieties of schooling models available increases, the Stockholm syndrome fades. In an environment of options—as choices are made deliberately—praise of any one model becomes more influential and meaningful to others.

Finally realize that . . .

32

....

Schools are designed to create both winners and losers.

Schools and their classrooms are as competitive as any sport. By design, they rely on a motivational and management system in which there must be winners and there must be losers.

Specifically, schools pit students against each other to get them to participate in their programs rather than use more aspirational and productive techniques.

Classes and other activities aren't just graded; they are graded on a curve, with percentages of students being pushed into the highest and lowest categories. And the schools recognize and otherwise reward the "best" students in the form of public honors (including publishing the Honor Roll in the local papers) and one-on-one teacher praise, even to the point of assigning moral virtue.

Among the ecosystem implications of this system are these:

- The most successful students are legitimate threats to everyone else. Many students are taught to logically resent the smartest students. Some of the smartest students even respond to the social pressure not to perform well.

- Students are motivated to help only other students who are, in the ranking system, permanently below them.

- As with athletes doping, the payoff for students to cheat becomes increasingly worth the risk for some.

But there are more macro implications. True, one can argue that life is competitive and that students might as well get used to it. Fair enough. But consider:

- Many top students are motivated to excel primarily by maintaining their "top student" status. Thus any politician who advocates using schools as a vehicle to attain broad citizenship excellence is completely missing the inherent nature of schools.

- This also means that (massive amounts of) taxpayer dollars are supporting institutions that will necessarily classify and even create "losers" of at least a third of all students. Resources are being dedicated to creating an institutional underclass.

- Many of the skills rewarded in schools do not have productive-world implications. We could just as well be giving the highest moral status to the best jugglers.

Schools are designed to be compulsory and highly competitive, and they take up an increasingly large percentage of childhood and thus crowd out other nonschool activities. What can possibly go wrong with that model?

Part Four: Customization

33

In education, customization is important like air is important.

When people look back at the current education-industrial model, they will be dumbfounded by its lack of customization. The truth is that children are much more diverse in makeup than are adults.

As time progresses, we will continue to discover still more ways in which children can be different from each other. Just some of the initial attributes in which they differ include:

- Facility with numbers
- Facility with words
- Facility with foreign languages
- Facility with music
- Facility with peers
- Facility with authority
- Tolerance for being separated from parents

- Tolerance for being separated from siblings
- Tolerance for being separated from home
- Effective discipline approaches
- Effective motivational approaches
- Productivity when working alone
- Productivity when working with peers
- Need for exercise
- Need for movement when processing thoughts and ideas
- Need for sleep
- Need for food
- Need for aesthetically pleasing surroundings
- Need for social accord
- Time of day the person is most able to produce written work
- Time of day the person is most able to absorb new concepts
- Time of day to most accurately take tests

This rule seems to be both the most self-evident and the most disregarded. Schools today tend to wish these differences didn't exist, and they even work hard to get rid of them.

It is much more measurable and cost-effective to employ just a few fundamental approaches to education. But applying these broad schedules and media and techniques necessarily means unbelievable tedium and ineffectiveness for all students. Worse, it creates a sense of "not fitting in" for almost all of them.

Some people argue that students need to learn to conform to a single model so that they can "fit in." Instead, each student simply needs to figure out how to be his or her best in order to excel.

This leads to the realization that . . .

34

....

There is no one answer to how to educate a child. There may not be any answers.

The bad news is that there is no answer to how best to educate a child.

Every child is different. Every home context is different. The notion of "one path for education" is orders of magnitude more absurd than "everyone should drive the same kind of car."

It gets worse. Education is a young science, not yet out of its own adolescence. There is not the scientific rigor and history of physics, engineering, or biology. Educational theory makes economics look accurate. And it gets murkier still.

Let's say it takes 30 years to get a feeling for whether the process used to raise a child was right. And let's also say the world fundamentally changes, even just in terms of technology and careers, about every 10 years. You can see the problem.

Anyone who says they have the answer to the best way of raising children is lying. In fact, they probably want something from you.

The good news is that if you understand the bad news, you can avoid the charlatans with their overconfident promises, detailed yet inflexible processes, desire to eliminate competitive approaches, and fear peddling. Then, and only then, can you really begin to educate.

Which means that you should . . .

35

....

Be what schools pretend to be, not what schools are.

If you read schools' mission statements, you have to be impressed with their clarity of vision. Nowhere do they write, "We teach pre-calculus better than anyone else." Instead, they write something like, "We strive to serve the individual needs of each student, developing all aspects of their personality, preparing them to be leaders of the future."

Of course, the bloom is quickly off the rose when you see what public and private schools actually do. But that is just quibbling.

So, if you feel you have to take one thing from schools to emulate, don't take their schedules, or methodologies, or teacher-student relationships, or curricula, or textbooks.

Take their brochures.

This is easier than you think if you think about . . .

36

....

Fifteen models that are better for childhood learning than schools are.

Here are at least fifteen learning models for communities and individuals to consider that are better for childhood learning than traditional schools' lectures, papers, tests, grades, and transcripts.

- Summer camps: Be engaged outdoors, not coerced indoors.

- Libraries/YMCA or YWCA/Boys and Girls Clubs of America: Pick what interests you today.

- Internships and volunteering: Spend time with smarter people to understand what work is and can be, and then do meaningful work by helping or tutoring others.

- Family trips: Go on short- and longer-term journeys with the people who matter most.

- Pick-up sports: Experience existential play and find balance.

- Organized sports leagues/chess competitions/spelling bees/multiplayer computer games: Raise your own game performance level through competition.

- Self-Study: Explore a passion.

- Music/art class: Learn at the right pace from a tutor or in a small group.

- Community theater/improv: Join a disparate group of people under a strong leader to pursue a common and entertaining goal.

- Book clubs/discussion groups: Learn *to be* as well as *to know*.

- Writing groups/photography clubs: Peer review helps individuals improve their outputs.

- Garage band/moviemaking/start-up business: Peer-to-peer small groups, self-organized and centered around common interests, can generate rewarding collective output.

- World of Warcraft/Facebook/Blogs: Learn *to do* and learn *to be* remotely.

- 4-H/Future Farmers of America: Learn stewardship, leadership, and authenticity.

The current model of school, in which "tests" and "accountability" are all-important, means that teachers are financially motivated to dissuade students from all of the alternatives in that list.

Having said that, these alternatives, which have always existed in the shadow of schools, either to support schools or to fit in the cracks around schools, are starting to evolve to meet the needs of home- and unschoolers as well. For example, libraries are starting to host gatherings of home- and unschoolers around such issues as environmentalism, current affairs, internships, or starting their own businesses, not just tutoring sessions on homework help and test prep.

Expanding this list of learning models, and others, will eventually help all students, including those in industrial schools. The long-term influence of home- and unschoolers on these "better models" will evolve and hone the approaches necessary to achieve the comprehensive education goals of any nation.

Regardless of the approach, one should . . .

37

....

Feed passions and embrace excellence.

No matter what his or her age, when a child has a serious and productive interest in something, do anything possible to feed it. Be the perfect enabler.

Drive anywhere. Fly anywhere. Rearrange schedules. Get or otherwise provide access to the supplies and props (and animals and vehicles and equipment and ...). Find the experts, communities, even mentors. (Eventually you'll want to find people who can provide real and credible feedback.)

Just as importantly, protect the child from the trivial work inevitably and often mindlessly and reflexively foisted on him or her by others. A year absolutely dedicated to a single area of deep passion is better than the potpourri of modern curricula.

Some care needs to be taken not to subvert the

interest or overwhelm it. And admit your own humble status as not being an expert.

Childhood passion based on curiosity and real interest is one of the most powerful forces. This is what eventually shapes industries and nations.

Such customizing of a child's learning also means appreciating that . . .

38

....

Children learn unevenly,
even backwards.

The industrial school model is that of even progress. There is the first grade. Then there is the second. Then the third. Students are expected to build their knowledge in parallel across a variety of topics in a linear and additive way.

The reality could not be more different. Learning abilities and usable knowledge bases are wildly different from student to student.

Imagine you are on a scooter, and your assignment is to move ahead 10 feet. You would do this easily, and might get praise for doing it so well.

Now imagine you are in the same class, but you are in a helicopter for the first time. You are told to move forward.

You press a random lever and your rotors spin loudly. You go up and then come crashing down. The other students on their scooters look at you angrily; you are causing a scene. The instructor tells you to move forward again but reduces the goal to only 5 feet, noting your difficulty. You press something else and lurch backwards. Now the instructor is furious. Meanwhile, a red light is flashing in your cockpit.

The final rub in this analogy, of course, is that a helicopter is a much more powerful and valuable vehicle. Ten years later, you are going to want the helicopter saving you where the scooter could not.

We are so much more diverse from person to person, and even month to month, than we have internalized. And our tools keep changing on us: scooter 1 month, helicopter the next, perhaps a cinder block the month after that. Some tasks are effortless, some are arduous, and still others are impossible.

Any structure that does not embrace the chaotic diversity of talents is doomed to a lower common denominator approach. Ultimately, along the way that approach creates a corrupt moral framework around temporary abilities measured by incomplete short-term standards.

As you acknowledge this, you will be asking yourself . . .

39

....

Five subjects a day? Really?

Many school curricula use a model of five or six "classes" taught throughout the day, broken up into even chunks and combined with lunch and other breaks. This makes planning the movement of large numbers of children possible.

But if you didn't have a school structure—if you were instead dedicated to each student's learning—how many subjects would you teach?

The answer would probably be something like this: "It depends on the day, student, and subject. Maybe one. Or one hundred. Or zero."

Having said that, a default broad schedule like the one adopted by most schools makes sense for some who crave a bit of order. For such individuals, the most basic is most likely the best: have one morning subject and one afternoon subject.

And speaking of subjects . . .

40

....

Maturing solves a lot of problems.

I have the perfect business model. Be a childhood psychologist. Give a 100 percent guarantee of improvement in behavior. But there is one catch. No matter when the child signs up for your program, he or she has to stay through to the age of seventeen and a half.

The truth here is that maturation is magic. Irrational teenagers do become rational. Calmness and focus return.

All of childhood is filled with times of equilibrium and disequilibrium. Friends can be charmed by a 10-year-old and sing his or her praises (and sing the praises of the parents for doing such a great job of childrearing). Those same friends can be repelled by the same child just a year later. Savvy parents practice the art of timing the periodic visits of distant relatives carefully.

Children's bodies do each have their own clock. Each clock just may not match the expectations of the structures around the children.

It is far too easy for anyone raising a child to falsely attribute external events as the cause for internal swings. The most manipulative of behaviors, meanwhile, is for any organization that deals with children to take credit for the good swings and to blame external forces for the bad ones.

·

Part Five: Community

41

Socialize your children.
Just don't use schools to do it.

Children need to be socialized. They need to spend time with peers and adults that is both positive and productive. They are capable of building relationships and habits that can last a lifetime.

Given that, which of the following school environments meet the need for developing good socialization skills:

- The bus stop?
- The bus ride?
- The hallways?
- The classrooms?
- The playground?
- The cafeteria?
- The restrooms?

- The locker rooms?
- The gym?
- The athletic fields?

For many people, the answer may be *none of the above*. Schools seem to provide a variety of unhealthy social situations that are more likely to build scar tissue and resentment than success. Sharp elbows and drugs and sexual pressure abound.

Socialization has to happen despite school, and perhaps even to compensate for school, rather than through school. So it may be more accurate to think of any school social time not as a solution to the need for socialization, but as negative social time that requires more positive get-togethers to overcome the bad influence.

And speaking of good socializing practices . . .

42

Grouping students by the same age is just a bad idea.

The education-industrial complex is structured around organizing children by age. This is a bad idea for so many reasons.

First among them is that this notion is based on a false assumption that young people of the same age have roughly the same skill level in subjects across the curriculum. Clearly, this is not the case. Even the maturity level between genders is a schism. Likewise, different students with different interests and interest levels have wildly different abilities.

But grouping by age remains an "objective" easy criterion, one whose inaccuracy has done nothing to minimize its use.

More importantly, putting children in groups of "peers," organizing students to emphasize their social sameness, necessarily forces them to emphasize and exaggerate their differences. Stop for a moment to imagine the Kafkaesque nightmare of being part of a community that was organized because someone thought you all were interchangeable. You would spend a lot of energy differentiating yourself through your actions and your dress and ultimately through forming social cliques.

Monocultures don't work. They are the product of a dated manufacturing mentality of mass production, and are seldom found in nature. That is why the waste from a deer in the wild enriches the soil, whereas sewage from a massive pig farm causes a health risk to the communities that live downstream.

In childhood learning, diversity of ages and experiences allows everyone to find their strengths in a vibrant ecosystem. Adults and kids should interact. Older people can mentor younger ones. Younger people can use their strength and vitality, each of them wanting to contribute and find a role to fill uniquely.

This means that you should . . .

43

....

Minimize "the drop-off."

Nothing more typifies modern parenting than "the drop-off." Parents are addicted to outsourcing their children to paid (or volunteer) caregivers. They drop off their sons and daughters at birthday parties, little league, and of course, schools.

(As an aside, this behavior predictably results in *the list of instructions*. The parents leave the caregiver not only with their ward but also with ever-increasingly long lists of do's and don'ts. This makes the parents believe they are still doing their job. The cycle is complete when the parents proceed to grade the caregiver after the fact. The experienced caregiver smiles and nods and placates and ignores.)

Every drop-off should be questioned. Over time, drop-offs should be minimized.

Parents might, for example, stay with their child at the party rather than use it as an opportunity to do their own errands. Likewise, the errands themselves, if annotated for a child, provide some of the richest learning opportunities.

It may be that this "drop-off" behavior has most enabled the education-industrial complex and, if reversed, can help parents reduce their reliance on it.

And if you don't drop off, you can . . .

44

Increase exposure to non–authority figure adults.

In the age of "the drop-off," parents often unfortunately look at any adults willing to spend time with their offspring as potential stand-in caregivers. This is robbing children of one of the greatest learning opportunities— time with the non–authority figure adult.

Children should be given the opportunity to spend peer time with as many adults as possible. Adults in this "peer mode," instead of bearing the enormous burden of worrying about safety and nutrition and other liabilities, can be humorous, at ease, and honest. With parents in earshot, the other adults can be role models and endless sources of insight, not just the "person in charge *du jour*." These relationships may evolve into apprentice and/or mentor models, but let such adults and children spend a long time just as friends.

Part Six: Credit

45

....

Tests don't work. Get over it. Move on.

During the latter part of the 19th century and the first half of the 20th, the number of doctors rose dramatically. This despite the fact that doctors did not help their patients, and in many cases, they made things worse. There was a desperate *need* for doctors that overwhelmed the reality.

That brings us to today's school-based technique of testing. The vision is to have concentrated moments of pure evaluation, where students are asked to demonstrate what they know.

And we want tests to work so badly. We love the idea of a simple-to-deploy, objective mechanism that can sort, motivate, and diagnose—the equivalent of quality control at a car manufacturing plant looking for defects.

The only problem is that tests do everything wrong.

Tests only test the test taker's ability to prepare for

and take tests. For example, there is no skill worth having that can be measured through a multiple-choice exam.

Worse, tests emphasize exactly the wrong skills. They emphasize the memorization of massive amounts of facts that neurologically have a half-life of about 12 hours. They focus on short-term rewards through cramming to compensate for a failure in long-term development of value. It is no wonder we have financial meltdowns caused by successful students.

We have to swallow a hard pill. The issue is not how do we make tests better? Or how can we have more or different types of tests? Or how do we arrange for more parts of a school program (such as a teacher's worth) to be based on tests?

The reality is, tests don't work except as a blunt control-and-motivation mechanism for the classroom, the academic equivalent of MSG or sugar in processed food. In place of schools as testing centers, we have to begin imagining and setting up learning environments that involve no tests at all, that rely on real assessment and the creation of genuine value instead.

There is an alternative, because . . .

46

....

The future is portfolios, not transcripts.

Schools and students live and die by transcripts—the one or two pages that list all the classes taken and the grades received. File cabinets of transcripts create a uniform, easy-to-compare mechanism to stack rank the relative worth of students.

Or at least they try. The truth is, those transcripts compress or outright lose more information and insight than they retain.

Instead, the future is student portfolios. Portfolios are skimmable but dense collections of media that show off a person's capabilities and passions. They can exist in both electronic and paper form.

Many students at graduate levels, as well as professionals, already use portfolios, of course. Artists, architects, and producers, as just a few examples, all have portfolios that they shape over time and present to potential partners or customers.

The best student portfolios must feature these attributes, among others, if they are to be of most value:

- The collections of work will cover years, even decades. Only over time can the threads of passions and other themes be drawn.

- They will be multimedia, using words, photographs, and video clips.

- They will include external validation, where appropriate. This may include awards, references in local papers, and letters of thanks from recipients.

Portfolios have one inherent risk, however. The presentation of an activity can become more salient than the activity itself. The person who spends months in the maintenance of her favorite hiking trail should not be overshadowed by someone who spends 1 hour on a great photo shoot. Authenticity and accomplishment over time, rather than slickness, must remain the key to a university or an employer using portfolios as part of an assessment process.

In the future, people will increasingly present this type of portfolio, whether applying to a college or for a new job. They would do well to heed the warning in the preceding paragraph. One of the biggest beneficiaries of this shift will be the college admissions and HR people who can see applicants once again as actual people and make judgments accordingly.

And portfolios are easier if you . . .

47

....

Keep a focused journal.

One of the most powerful tools for developing a new situational awareness is accurately and comprehensively recording something relevant. For example, for 1 month:

- Write down everything you eat, in terms of calories.
- Write down everything you spend.
- Take a picture from the exact same spot of a construction site. Or a garden in spring.
- Measure the rainfall per day.
- Record the number of steps you take each day.
- Record the number and types of commercials during a consistent half hour of television.
- Record the number and makes of cars that

go through red lights during a consistent
half hour.

This collapses time and draws attention to patterns
that otherwise would be noise. It also helps overcome
the subjectivity and superstition of personal experience.
But also remember to use . . .

48

....

Use technology as assessment.

Playing tennis without a net is great for getting comfortable with the sport, but not for rigorously developing new skills. Assessment raises our game. But the traditional means schools use for assessment—tests—measure only the increasingly useless ability to memorize. What should real assessment look like?

Technology may provide an answer by making available communities and social systems with measurable rubrics. Consider some targets:

- For Twitter, how many followers do you have? Can you get to 100? 1,000?

- For a blog, how many other blogrolls can you be on? Or can you write thirty entries that you are willing to share with the world? How many hits can you get? How many followers? Can you get cited on other blogs? How many?

- Can you make $20 profit on eBay? How about $200?

Some people argue that these assessments are not pure enough. They can be gamed and otherwise manipulated by students to get better scores than their actual skills or work effort would warrant. Perhaps.

But for those who think that tests and term papers do not involve gaming, I can only respectfully disagree. Every assessment can be gamed. (The best students are often the best at gaming.) The trick is to make that part of the learning.

More importantly, there is a trap that we should at least recognize. Those defending the current educational system will predictably demand that every new approach to education should meet a threshold no old approach even comes close to meeting. It is a near-perfect deflection strategy. But it is ultimately a bluff that needs to be called out.

And then there is the biggest assessment of all . . .

49

....

College: the hardest no-win decision your family may ever make.

If you were a perfect marketer of a service, how would you structure your business? How did General Motors sell cars so well in the 1950s, for example?

- First, you would try to position your product as being a necessity (you don't want people trying to figure out its value) and as being time sensitive (you advertise that the "sale ends Thursday" because you wouldn't want people to put off the buying decision).

- Second, you would not only sell your primary service but also a stream of little ones. You would offer generous loan programs to spread out payments over ever-longer terms.

- Third, you would offer a bit of choice, between three and five alternatives, to give consumers the illusion of their free will and control. You would offer a high-end luxury version, with the inherent promise of elitism. You might even have some "if you qualify" clauses. You would also offer a low-end, basic functionality. And you would offer a few in-the-middle options so people could get something that allows them to express their personality.

Fast-forward to decision-making about undergraduate college today. The education-industrial complex wants to sell as many school hours as possible. That's their business. So they want parents and students to assume, when those students reach the end of high school, that they will spend the next 4 years in college. The decision is not "if," "why," or "when," but "which," and what they are buying is not only the big service but also as many add-ons as possible.

The first truth is that this is a big decision. It is a decision that has many pros and cons: from credibility, mainstreaming, lifelong friendships, and pre-reqs for worthwhile advanced degrees on the one hand to binge drinking, staggering debt and subsequent indentured servitude, high drop out rates (especially for males), aimlessness, and protracted adolescence on the other.

Selecting a college is also a different decision than it

was 30 years ago, or 20, or 10. College costs have been rising faster than the economy and inflation for decades.

Meanwhile, the predictive value of a college education is going down as corporations are increasingly less likely to provide extended training resources and opportunities to new grads. This is a result of the average length of tenure for new employees going ever downward.

The second truth is that the economics around traditional 4-year universities will change as fundamentally in this decade as the economics changed for newspapers in the last decade. With the presence of online universities, growing virtual communities, high-value open-source content, and emerging portfolio and other "credit for real world experience" programs, the illusion of the inevitability of a conventional undergraduate education is finally shattered and the value-proposition is challenged.

For many, graduating from college has changed from the opportunity enabling of the past to a Pyrrhic victory today. But things will continue to change, and this time for the better. In the near future, college will not be one big no-win choice. It will be a series of worthwhile and exciting little choices made over decades.

Part Seven: [Day] Care

50

....

Outdoors beats indoors.

When in formal learning mode, students should spend as much time outside as possible. Our grandparents were right. Be active. Walk through woods and cities. Sit on rocks and curbs, not chairs that cramp.

Rain and snow aren't bad things. They are good things.

Inside is, of course, more controlled. It is predictable. Activities can be scheduled more predictably indoors. Factories are all inside. No wonder schools like inside so much. But it is dead. Children need change and movement.

Outdoors, by contrast, requires flexibility. It eschews schedules. But it rewards with density of stimulation and calmness of order and organization.

And we can . . .

51

....

Walk a lot.

The predominant academic milieu should be walking. When walking, children can talk. They can think. They can see the world around them at the right scale (better than biking or driving).

And when walking routinely, children can see the slight changes—a new car, a new roof, new spring growth or fall colors, a new sale at a shop, a new family member moving in—that herald real milestones or interesting decisions. This can and should be more relevant, and even more educational, than the rise and fall of the Egyptian empire.

Taking advantage of walking is easier if you . . .

52

....

Under-schedule to take advantage of the richness of life.

One myth is, the busier a student is, the more he or she learns. Children's days, the common thinking goes, should be scheduled tightly to maximize the amount of formal instruction and rehearsals and extracurricular events.

But when a schedule is a bit more porous, it can allow for happenstance. Here's a real example.

A homeschooler and parent are driving in their car and see two local police cars. They slow down then stop. They sit and watch as a third police car comes. The student and parent get out of the car. Then a state police officer arrives with dogs. A crowd is forming. People start talking. There was, people are saying, a person who left a suicide note and is now missing. An ambulance and a fire engine arrive. Then a thundering Life-Star helicopter. The paramedics swarm; the person is found. The local news arrives, interviewing people. Moments later, in a cloud of dust, the Life-Star helicopter flies off to a local hospital.

When there is room to explore, there is the opportunity to watch the real world evolve in a way that has so much more resonance than a textbook or museum exhibit or teenage novel or Hollywood blockbuster.

Life is educational. But only if you let it be.

Which brings up the biggest issue . . .

53

....

Parents care more than any institution about their children.

Every rule, every law, every arrangement between institution and parent has to agree on the most fundamental presumption: it is the parents who care the most about their children.

One virulent meme that spreads through so many schools and legislative bodies—namely, that parents get in the way and are incapable of making intelligent decisions for their children—is the defense mechanism of institutions that cannot change and is as corrosive as any other form of discrimination. Worse, it can become self-fulfilling in some cases.

Which leads to both the most and the least controversial rule . . .

54

Children should be raised by people who love them.

Children need to spend as much time as possible around the adults who love them. Ideally, this means parents and grandparents. It can also mean the right aunt or uncle.

This is because children need to be around adults who care about their long-term future. Not their behavior next week, or next season, but 10 or 15 years from now.

The alternatives are necessarily grim. Children become pawns in systems. They are used to meet contrived short-term goals. Teachers use them to get good test scores. Coaches use them to win games. They become the recipient of shortcuts. And their time is auctioned off.

Thankfully, increasing the hours spent per week or per day with a loving adult can happen incrementally.

Replace a babysitter with a grandparent. Bring a child along on an errand.

This is not always fun for either party, but the alternative of an unloving chaperone is almost always worse.

Conclusion

55

....

The only sustainable answer to the global education challenge is a diversity of approaches.

Collectively, the education-industrial complex, including legislators, school boards, school administrators, teachers, and school vendors, displays many of the behaviors of a monopoly.

- Education services consume an increasingly larger share of a nation's GDP.

- Schools try to standardize as completely as possible the offerings. They are inflexible in dealing with customers and the community. Students are expected to change to meet the needs of the offering, as opposed to the other way around.

- Larger administrations are created in which

the middle layer does not teach but "manages."

- New teachers, because they do not have career options, are treated poorly (which often results in building deep resentment).

- Many staff members within the school system (similar to the fate of people who work within such traditional monopolies as AT&T decades ago or Facebook today) are overwhelmed by unrealistic and unfair burdens and expectations.

- Schools use internal metrics to evaluate success that no one outside of the school cares about.

- Schools heavily advertise and use PR to present themselves as local and caring.

- The primary functional goal of schools is to push children to consume more school hours (at the lowest possible cost of delivery), not to help them outside of the school.

- Schools truly believe their approach is the only approach.

- Schools seek to crush competition, such as vouchers and homeschooling. They will continue to employ powerful, legally enforced tools to penalize truancy and other "anti-school" behavior. Proxies will publish reports critical of new approaches.

And no monopoly has ever reformed itself. It is only through competition among entirely different entities that new ideas are nurtured and given the opportunity to evolve. (At first any new ideas are inevitably called "naive" and "impractical" or even "dangerous" by existing practitioners.)

Microsoft could not have happened if it were a part of IBM. Google and Amazon could not have happened if they were a part of Microsoft.

Similarly, a multinational food corporation would never "discover" the need for organic, minimally processed, locally grown agriculture on its own, no matter how many scientists and academics were on its payroll. It is only through independently minded and passionate people taking control of what they put into their own bodies that this "new" idea of healthy food could be developed, propagated, and ultimately mainstreamed.

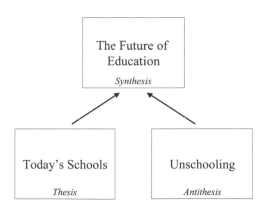

Which means that *significantly different approaches are possible in education.* And these new approaches will be necessary to enable the evolution of the education system to a new post-industrial future model.

This is critical, because the successor to today's schools must lead to significant improvements in the population's standard of living and our country's ability to meet competitive challenges. Camps and libraries and other organizations and content models will also play a greater complementary role in that new environment.

But it will not be the governments, or their school systems, or others of their institutions that will drive real innovation in reconstructing childhood education. It will be, as it already is, the homeschoolers and the unschoolers.

Afterword

It's time to tell the truth. Despite lots of well-meaning people and hundreds of billions of dollars, the Emperor of Education still has no clothes. The paradigm that children are widgets, little more than raw material for a conveyor-belt education designed to shape and form them, is misguided, and no amount of money or rules or laws will make it work. It is a system that is as morally flawed as it is ineffective.

Children are not raw materials to be made into productive citizens by "the system." Children are beautiful living souls, as much angel as devil, each deserving of a hero's journey through life, where they can strive and fail and grow up to change the world.

The innovation in education we need is not going to come from an Industrial Revolution–age educational paradigm. The type of people who gave us schools filled with rows of industrialized lockers, Pavlovian bells ringing on the hour, and teachers' unions that care far more about tenure than nurturing the dreams of children are not the ones who can suddenly become the leaders of educational innovation.

That means the future belongs to—and depends on—people like you and me. People who are willing to dive into the messy, chaotic, joyful, ever-changing world of unschooling to create the ideas and innovations that will topple the old regime.

Sound a little revolutionary? Well, perhaps it's time for that.

Ready to join the revolution? If so, here are some next steps you can take.

1. If you are a teacher or an administrator, learn more about the Industrial Age roots of our modern assembly-line schools. Explore alternative approaches and philosophies, some rooted in classical education, others taking advantage of the latest in disruptive technologies. *A Thomas Jefferson Education* by Oliver DeMille, *The Underground History of American Education* by John Gatto, and *NurtureShock* by Po Bronson and Ashley Merryman are three powerful resources and are some of my favorites.

2. If you are a parent with young children, read these same books and investigate the world of Montessori, where "learning to be"

and "learning to do" and a deep respect for children are thoroughly interwoven into the curriculum.

Also check out some of the newest offerings in game-based software for basic skills, like DreamBox for math (www.dreambox.com) or Rosetta Stone for language (www.rosettastone.com). Take time to investigate project-based and student-centered learning at schools like the Acton Academy (www.actonacademy.org).

3. If you are a politician or education reformer, explore online project-based alternatives like K[12]'s distance-based education (www.k12.com), and read Harvard Business School Professor Clay Christensen's *Disrupting Class* and Clark Aldrich's *Learning by Doing* to see why the world of education is changing faster than you think.

Also, please take some time to dig deeply into the world of homeschooling. I promise that you will not find a collection of religious and political nuts but brave and committed parents engaged in exciting educational experiments.

Above all, each and every one of us must keep asking questions. Why? Because in education, lives are always on the line, and it's up to people like you—people with courage—to begin to say aloud, "The old way isn't working." It's time to dive into the world of unschooling to find the leaders of tomorrow.

Jeff Sandefer
Winter 2010

Places to Start

Here are lists of the specific rules described in this book that have direct and straightforward action implications for school administrators, parents of children in traditional schools, and policy makers. For those who want to bring about change, begin with these rules, which are listed according to the best places to start.

For school administrators:

46. The future is portfolios, not transcripts. (Page 117)

29. Homework helps school systems, not students. (Page 71)

16. Embrace all technologies. (Page 39)

11. Use microcosms as much as possible in learning programs. (Page 29)

24. Teaching is leadership. Most teaching is bad leadership. (Page 59)

39. Five subjects a day? Really? (Page 99)

15. If you care about learning, start with food. (Page 37)

For parents of children in traditional schools:

12. Internships, apprenticeships, and interesting jobs beat term papers, textbooks, and tests. (Page 31)

13. Include meaningful work. (Page 33)

25. Expose more, teach less. (Page 61)

43. Minimize "the drop-off." (Page 109)

44. Increase exposure to non–authority figure adults. (Page 111)

14. Create and use periods of reflection. (Page 35)

30. Every day, adults are role models of learning (whether or not they want to be). (Page 73)

For policy makers:

55. The only sustainable answer to the global education challenge is a diversity of approaches. (Page 143)

45. Tests don't work. Get over it. Move on. (Page 115)

4. Twenty-five critical skills are seldom taught, tested, or graded in high school. (Page 13)

3. Learn something because you need it or because you love it. (Page 11)

18. One computer + one spreadsheet software program = math curricula. (Page 43)

33. In education, customization is important like air is important. (Page 83)

Twitter hash tags

Twitter your progress. Broadly, use #unschoolin-grules. As you work on any of these issues, use #un-rulesXX as the Twitter hash tag, where XX is the rule number. For example, if you are working on the issue of developing portfolios (Rule 46), use #unrules46 as the Twitter hash tag.

For ongoing news go to the *Unschooling Rules* web-site, located at www.unschoolingrules.com, for addi-tional entries, discussions, and news.

About the Author

 Clark Aldrich is a global education thought leader, labeled a guru by *Fortune Magazine*. He works with corporate, military, government, and academic organizations at both the board level and as a hands-on implementer.

Clark's projects have been patent winning and earned millions globally. He is the author of four books published by Wiley and scores of articles, is the recipient of numerous industry awards, created dozens of educational simulations (including the most popular leadership simulation in the world), was the founder of Gartner's eLearning coverage, and has a degree in cognitive science from Brown University. His work has been featured in hundreds of sources, including CBS, ABC, *The New York Times*, *Wall Street Journal*, CNN, NPR, CNET, *Business 2.0*, *BusinessWeek*, and *U.S. News & World Report*.